WITHDRAWN

Laura Bush

Jennifer Strand

abdopublishing.com

Published by Abdo Zoom™, PO Box 398166, Minneapolis, Minnesota 55439. Copyright © 2018 by Abdo Consulting Group, Inc. International copyrights reserved in all countries. No part of this book may be reproduced in any form without written permission from the publisher. Abdo Zoom™ is a trademark and logo of Abdo Consulting Group, Inc.

Printed in the United States of America, North Mankato, Minnesota
052017
092017

THIS BOOK CONTAINS
RECYCLED MATERIALS

Cover Photo: Krisanne Johnson/George Bush Presidential Library/Library of Congress
Interior Photos: Krisanne Johnson/George Bush Presidential Library/Library of Congress, 1; Valentina Petrov/Shutterstock Images, 4; Shutterstock Images, 5, 8–9, 13, 18; Courtesy George W. Bush Presidential Library and Museum, 6, 10, 14, 15, 17; Seth Poppel/Yearbook Library, 7; Harry Cabluck/AP Images, 11; Pat Sullivan/AP Images, 12; Mike Derer/AP Images, 16; Carol M. Highsmith/The Lyda Hill Texas Collection of Photographs in Carol M. Highsmith's America Project/Library of Congress, 19
Cover Photo: Krisanne Johnson/George Bush Presidential Library/Library of Congress

Editor: Emily Temple
Series Designer: Madeline Berger
Art Direction: Dorothy Toth

Publisher's Cataloging-in-Publication Data
Names: Strand, Jennifer, author.
Title: Laura Bush / by Jennifer Strand.
Description: Minneapolis, MN : Abdo Zoom, 2018. | Series: First ladies | Includes bibliographical references and index.
Identifiers: LCCN 2017931130 | ISBN 9781532120152 (lib. bdg.) | ISBN 9781614797265 (ebook) | 9781614797821 (Read-to-me ebook)
Subjects: LCSH: Bush, Laura Welch, 1946- --Juvenile literature. | Presidents spouses--United States--Biography--Juvenile literature.
Classification: DDC 973.931/092 [B]--dc23
LC record available at http://lccn.loc.gov/2017931130

Table of Contents

Laura Bush was a First Lady
of the United States.

George W. Bush is her husband. They guided the United States through difficult times.

Laura was born on
November 4, 1946.

She grew up in Texas.
She was a good student.

Leader

After college Laura worked in schools. She liked working with children. She taught them that reading is important.

Laura married George W. Bush in 1977. She worked on his **campaigns**.

In 1994 he became **governor** of Texas.

Laura became the First Lady of Texas. She raised money for a **literacy program**.

The money bought books for schools. The program also helped kids learn to read.

Laura became First Lady in 2001.

That year **terrorists** attacked the United States. It was a hard time. She worked with her husband to unite the country.

She supported parents and children after the attack. Laura continued to support literacy, too.

She worked to help teachers. She taught parents that reading to kids is important.

17

Legacy

The Bushes left the
White House in 2009.

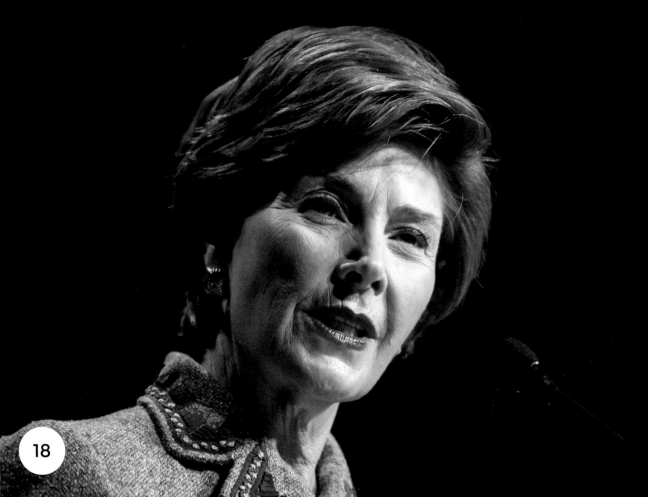

Laura Bush is remembered for supporting literacy in families. Today she and her husband work to promote women's health.

Laura Bush

Born: November 4, 1946

Birthplace: Midland, Texas

Husband: George W. Bush

Years Served: 2001–2009

Known For: Laura Bush was a US First Lady. She supported literacy and education.

Key Dates

1946: Laura Lane Welch is born on November 4.

1968: Laura starts her first teaching job. She later works as a librarian.

1977: George W. Bush and Laura Welch are married on November 5.

1995: As Texas First Lady, Laura begins her work for literacy programs.

2001–2009: Laura Bush is First Lady of the United States. George W. Bush serves as president.

Glossary

campaign - the process of trying to get voted into office.

governor - a person who is the head of a state in the United States.

literacy - the ability to read and write.

program - a plan of action for achieving something, such as improved literacy.

terrorist - someone who uses violence and threats to scare people, usually in an effort to change something.

Booklinks

For more information on
Laura Bush, please visit
abdobooklinks.com

Zoom In on Biographies!

Learn even more with the Abdo Zoom
Biographies database. Check out
abdozoom.com for more information.

Index